EXodus

Mike
DeVries
and
Troy
Murphy

The Sacred Journey

"No Limits" Discipleship Series

Barefoot Ministries
Kansas City, Missouri

To the founders of South County United.
We are so blessed and thankful to be in community with
you. May God continue the "sacred journey" He started
in all of us as we studied the Book of Exodus together.

Contents

Acknowledgments

Thanks

To our wives, Jamie and Tricia. We are better men because of you. You have been, and will always be, everything.

To Jeff Edmondson, Jim Hampton, and everyone at Barefoot Ministries. Partnership is a beautiful thing. Thanks for believing in this project and making a reality the dream of so many.

To our God. You are the reason we live and breathe. You are our Creator and Sustainer. Thank You for taking us on the "sacred journey" into Your heart.

Entering In #1

The Awakening

June 2, 1990. It's a day that I'll never forget, a day that changed everything. Ever have those moments or places that you look back on knowing that from that moment on you'll never be the same, that there's no way you could ever go back to what you were before? June 2, 1990, was that day for me. Everything I knew before that day was gone, eclipsed in a moment of awakening. What happened on June 2? Simple—my wedding day.

June 2, 1990, I entered the day a single person and left the day a married man. What took place, the events of that 24-hour period, left me changed forever. I could never go back to what I was on June 1 no matter how hard I tried. The encounter changed me, and I awakened to a new reality in my life—a new journey. I was now married to one of God's most amazing creations: my wife, Jamie.

Our lives are filled with those moments, moments that change us forever, moments that we look back on and say, "From that moment on, I awakened to a new reality, a new way of living, a new insight into God or myself." Those moments are markers for us, markers of awakening.

Exodus—Awakening to the Sacred Journey

The Book of Exodus is all about awakenings. It's about God taking His people, the Israelites, on a journey that will awaken and forge their identity as a nation. It's about a man named Moses, awakening to a new relationship with the God of the universe and a new relationship with the people of God as their leader. It's a sacred journey of awakening that leaves Moses and his people changed forever.

The Book of Exodus, which literally means "the departure," was a very important book to the Israelites. It recounted the story of God taking the Israelites out of Egypt, where they had been slaves for over 400 years, and bringing them into a land He had promised to them. It was a continuation of the Book of Genesis, where in the end we find the people of Israel mourning the death of Joseph in Egypt. The text forms some of the most rich and foundational theology of the nation of Israel—from the character and name of God, to the Passover, to the covenant and the Ten Words (the Ten Commandments), to idolatry and sin, to the thought of redemption and true worship.

Exodus at its core is a story about the God of the universe inviting a people to be His people, taking them out of slavery in Egypt and through the desert to the Promised Land. It's during this sacred journey through the desert that their identity as a people is changed. They leave as slaves but awaken to the reality that they're the chosen people of God. In the desert God reveals His character to them and initiates a covenant with His people, one that would forever change the way they saw themselves and God. Exodus is about awakening to a sacred journey, one that would shape the future of a nation and a person—Moses.

The Awakening of Moses

Moses is the chosen leader of this invitation into the heart of God for the nation. Raised in Pharaoh's household, Moses has learned the ways of the Egyptians. One day while out watching his people at hard labor, he sees an Egyptian beating a Hebrew, one of his own people. Filled with rage, he kills the Egyptian and buries him in the sand. Once the word gets out, Moses flees to a remote part of Egypt called Midian. It's in the desert in Midian, at the place called Mount Horeb, that Moses awakens to a new reality.

One day while tending the sheep of his father-in-law, Moses comes to Mount Horeb. On an ordinary day, going about his ordinary business, Moses is about to be awakened to the extraordinary. A bush catches on fire and doesn't burn up. A voice calls to Moses from within the flames. Moses is awakened to a God who is living and active, a God who is calling him, inviting him to be a part of what He's going to do in the lives of the Israelites.

Imagine the moment. The bush. The fire. The voice of God. "Do not come any closer," God says. "Take off your sandals, for the place where you are standing is holy ground" (Exodus 3:5). Moses obeys. In essence what God is saying to Moses is "Slow down. Don't rush into this encounter. I am God and altogether different than you. You need to acknowledge that by taking off your shoes, a slave in the presence of his Master."

Our Awakening

What God is saying to Moses is the same thing He says to you and me: *I want to speak to you. I want to use you as a part of My plan. But first you need to awaken to the fact of who I am and acknowledge who you are in My pres-*

ence. At the heart of the story is a man awakened by God and changed forever.

God has a plan, and His voice is calling: *Will you join Me on a sacred journey?* What will your answer be?

Your Awakening

Read Exodus 3:1-6 and reflect on the following:

1. What might Moses have been feeling at this point in his life?

2. How would you have responded?

3. What was God awakening in Moses?

4. What is God wanting to awaken in you?

Take a few moments and write a letter to God, expressing your thoughts and heart. Tell Him where you are spiritually and where you would like to see this sacred journey take you. What do you sense He wants to awaken in you? Give Him the freedom to lead and awaken in you all that He desires to.

Day 1

What Do You Do When Life Turns for the Worse?

Encounter the Word
Exodus 1:1-22

Explore the Word

Read Genesis 15:13. Genesis 15 is one of the most important chapters in God's Story—the Bible. Here we read about God making a covenant with Abram (later to be named Abraham), that through his bloodline will come a promised nation, the nation of Israel. We see in verse 13 that 400 years of this nation's life will not look very promising; in fact, it will be very bad.

Read Genesis 50:22-26. This is the end of the Book of Genesis, and the 400 years are almost over. We now hear God again reassure the brothers of Joseph that He is going to deliver them from this situation.

How does it feel when life doesn't go the way you planned? What do you do? For most of us, it's very difficult to see beyond tough circumstances. These tough times in life can look like failures, relational friction, family problems, injury, or even a death. No matter what it may be, it's difficult to see the forest for the trees. In other words, it's hard to get a bigger perspective of your whole life as it relates to God's plan. When we don't really know His big plan for our lives and those around us, it becomes very difficult to trust.

Jeremiah 29:11

"I know the plans I have for you," declares the LORD, "plans to prosper you and not to harm you, plans to give you hope and a future."

13

Live the Word

List the circumstances in your life that have caused you stress, worry, or frustration because they are not going according to your plan.

With that list, pray out loud and give to God your stress, worry, or frustration for each circumstance by saying, *God, I will trust in You for the plans of my life. Please take* . . . (Fill in with your list.)

Day 2

Who Picked Me?

Encounter the Word

Exodus 2:1-10

Explore the Word

In Exodus 1 we begin to see the story take shape. The Israelites are "fertile," which basically means they were multiplying so fast that it frightened the Egyptians. Pharaoh's decree to kill off all of the male babies was his plan for stopping this incredibly threatening growth. But as we've learned, God has a plan, and it will happen. Now Moses is one of these babies, and it's easy to miss the powerful irony that's unfolding. Moses' own sister, Miriam, is a slave girl to Pharaoh's daughter and is the one who rescues him from the river. Miriam is asked to get a Hebrew to nurse baby Moses, and she gets her mother, who is paid for it. Little does Pharaoh know that his own daughter is the instrument that God uses to save the Hebrews and destroy the Egyptians. God has a plan despite the adversity and picks Moses to be a key player in His story.

Live the Word

When life is not going as we planned, we can also doubt who we are and question whether God made a mistake by creating us. We can sometimes wonder if we're a part of God's story.

Read Psalm 139:1-16. Now read it and replace every "I," "me," and "my" with your name.

God not only picked you—He created you. He knows you and is unfolding a story in you.

Day 3

What Is Your Character Reflex?

Encounter the Word
Exodus 2:11-25

Explore the Word
The story of Moses jumps forward and places us years later where Moses is now grown and facing some very difficult situations. In 2:11 we find Moses confronted with an Egyptian beating a Hebrew. In 2:13 we find Moses in the middle of two Hebrew men fighting each other. In 2:17 we see a Moses in the middle of a band of shepherds harassing Midian's daughters. All three situations, oddly enough, deal with the issue of social injustice. We get a glimpse into the "character reflex" of Moses by how he responds to these three situations. This "character reflex" is not a new concept but one that fills the lives of many people in the Scriptures. It's true for us today. Usually a person's first reflex is a great gauge of what his or her character is like.

Live the Word
What would your character reflex have been in these situations? All too often our first reaction may not be what we think it would be. Many of us have grown up using the excuse "It's none of my business," but that reflex in itself is a glimpse of the condition of our character. The truth is that it is our business. When we became Christ followers, we received the Holy Spirit, who now is working to form our character reflex.

James 4:17
To one who knows the right thing to do and does not do it, to him it is sin (NASB).

Read John 14:25-27

Think of your first "character reflex" in the last month. What was your reflex like? Now, ask the Holy Spirit to take over and train your character reflex. Take a minimum of 30 minutes in a quiet place to listen to His direction.

Day 4

What Does God's Call Sound Like?

Encounter the Word
Exodus 3:1-22

Explore the Word

It has been about 40 years since Moses fled Egypt. We don't get much insight to what his life was like in these years, but we do know that he was shepherding sheep and soon to be shepherding a nation. Moses has no idea what lies ahead for his life. How does God call him? He creates something that catches his attention—a burning bush. Moses investigates and finds that it's not burning up! Can't you see God drawing him in? Then He calls him by name: "Moses! Moses!" (v. 4). Only when God gets Moses' attention does He reveal himself, His plan, and Moses' role within that plan.

Live the Word

If you're a Christ follower, then you've heard this call by God to come to Him (see John 10:3). What about the call to work for God in some way or role? Have you heard Him? A call from God can be a subtle, quiet whisper or a very big, obvious moment. It can come early in your life or when you're older. You might not have had this call yet on your life, but it doesn't mean you won't or that you will. God calls those He chooses for certain works, and others He calls to himself to simply live their lives fully for Him wherever they are. The important thing for us to remember is that we're all to follow the call Jesus gave at the end of His time on earth. Read Matthew 28:18-20. The Great Commission is the call we can know and respond to right where we are today. Take some time to memorize this call from Jesus. It is your call.

Day 5

Excuses, Excuses

Encounter the Word

Exodus 4:1-31

Explore the Word

Despite what we think or feel about God and His ways, we must come to the place of surrender and obedience. When God calls us, He's expecting us to obey. For most of us, this is easier said than done. What would your response have been to God if that was you at the burning bush? Moses' first reaction is to come up with all the excuses as to why he can't obey. Read the excuses, and describe what Moses was probably thinking and feeling.

3:11

3:13

4:1

4:10

4:13

Live the Word

We all would like to think that we're ready to respond to anything that God might have for us, but the truth is it can be very difficult. Read Hebrews 3:5-6. Spend some time in prayer, and ask God to build into you strength to respond when He calls.

What's Your Excuse?

Contemplation

Many of us living in North America have been so accustomed to our lifestyle that sometimes we can allow it to be the lens through which we understand Scripture. As you read through the Book of Exodus, pay close attention to the assumptions you might make about how it was based on a North Americanized culture and time. (For example, no freeways, no malls, no electricity, etc.)

Moses is born as an Israelite, a nation in slavery (1:1—2:10). Moses is spared and raised by Pharaoh, who has no idea that his stepson will be God's agent for delivering the Israelites out of slavery and the agent of destruction for the Egyptians. Moses begins to feel the tension inside his soul and reacts to the injustice by killing an Egyptian (2:11-17). He flees. Forty years later he gets the call from God through the burning bush and is asked to return to Egypt and be the messenger for God (3—4). The people, the place, and the plot have been established, and the Book of Exodus is that story.

Communication

"Coulda, shoulda, woulda" is a phrase most of us never want to say, because it means we missed something, something that was worth doing or going for. It was a moment of opportunity, maybe even a divine opportunity. They're the moments that God places in our lives where we have a choice —to obey or to disobey. Moses tries his best to wiggle out of this divine opportunity with excuses, but God does not let him. Many Christians today have opportunities yet find excuses for why they could not be obedient to that call. What about you? Have you sensed divine opportunities placed before you? When were they, and what did you do? Did you have excuses? What were they?

Community

The truth is that the Bible is full of stories of men and women who were faced with divine opportunities. Some obeyed, others did not. What's exciting for us today is that we're still experiencing these moments. The difference, however, is that we're often confronted with other opportunities, ones that usually get more of our attention and sometimes our lives. Opportunities like popularity, success in athletics or academics, wealth, power, and even pleasure are hard to turn down. Take some time to identify which of these worldly opportunities get most of your attention.

Moses' excuses have a similar ring to many of the excuses we or others might use today. "Who am I?" "Who are you?" "What if they don't believe me?" "What if I mess it up?" Which lead to the ultimate excuse of "I can't [or don't want to] do it." What are the excuses that you use most often when God asks something of you? As you look at those excuses, realize that none of them are reason not to follow God's call. Those excuses are disobedience. Spend some time confessing those excuses and asking God to forgive you. Then tell God that you're ready to obey any divine opportunity that He may place before you.

Compassion

As we're in community with other Christ followers, we can be great encouragers and supporters for others to respond in obedience to their divine opportunities. Are there any friends or family in your life that you can affirm or support as they're following a call from God? Call, write, or tell them how you feel about their decision, how it has motivated you, and encourage them to be faithful.

Day 1
Persecutions

Encounter the Word
Exodus 5:1-21

Explore the Word
After 400 years of this slavery in Egypt, the Hebrews have submitted so as not to make it any worse. Moses' and Aaron's first confrontation with Pharaoh does not go well and brings a heavier load on the Hebrews. This did not please Moses but probably did not surprise him. What came as a deeper source of anxiety and persecution is the anger and frustration that the Hebrew people have for Moses, who has made their oppression worse. Moses and Aaron are standing alone facing adversity from Pharaoh and the Hebrews.

Live the Word
Where does your persecution come from? It's obvious that we'll face adversity from those who don't believe (see John 2:5; 3:20), but where else can we face this kind of opposition? Read Matthew 5:10, 11 and 6:14. Take some time to reflect, and ask the Holy Spirit to reveal where you might have faced persecution from others, and forgive those who have persecuted you.

Day 2

When God Doesn't Meet Your Agenda

Encounter the Word
Exodus 5:22-23

Explore the Word
Moses is just beginning his journey of obedience with the Israelites and has no idea where it will lead them. We know what happens, so it can be easy for us when we read the story to assume that they know it, too. In chapter 5 we see the affliction that the Hebrews receive for Moses' action, which Moses did not plan for. In today's reading Moses is struck with the sobering reality that God is orchestrating the plans, doing things His way. You get the sense that Moses might even be angry in his questioning of God.

Live the Word
What do you do when God's ways don't match your own? Do you get angry with Him? Do you doubt Him? The Scriptures tell the story of a man named Job who had his life turned in a direction he never thought possible. He lost his sheep, cattle, camels, children, home, and his health—everything except his life. He and his friends begin to doubt God in Job 36—37. Read God's response in Job 38—41. Take time to pray, and ask God for forgiveness for any doubting, questioning, or anger you might have had or have today for something that's not gone your way.

Day 3

God's Promises

Encounter the Word

Exodus 6:1-27

Explore the Word

Have you ever had one of those talks when your parents
were so frustrated with you on an issue that they began
giving you the history of the family? It's the talk when
they say, "Sit down and let me tell you about what your
grandfather did." In a way, it's their way of giving us a
refresher course on the history of those before us and
how they made good on promises and commitments
made. In today's passage, Moses is getting a refresher
course on how God fulfills His promises. All of the ge-
nealogies given in Scripture are full of prophetic fulfill-
ment of a promise given. They assure us that God has
known all along what He was going to do and will fulfill
His promises.

Live the Word

Get a journal and take some time to write down some of
the promises God has made in Scripture. Write the ref-
erence next to each promise; write how God has fol-
lowed through on each promise with you.

Day 4

When God Is on Your Side

Encounter the Word

Exodus 6:28-7:7

Explore the Word

What takes place in today's reading is the ultimate confidence-builder for Moses. He's been giving excuses, doubting, and questioning God, and now God will empower him with a spiritual confidence that no one on earth can give or even has apart from God. Look at Exodus 7:1—"See, I have made you like God to Pharaoh." It's not that Moses is a god but that he's made "like God." In other words, God made Pharaoh see a part of himself through Moses.

Live the Word

This spiritual transformation, of others seeing God through us, is a central theme in the New Testament. When we accept the gift of Jesus' death and resurrection for us, we are filled with the Holy Spirit, who makes us like a light in a dark world. Then people will also begin to see God in us.

Read Matthew 5:13-16 and John 3:20-22. Sin can darken that light within us, and people most likely will not see Jesus through us. Spend some time confessing any sin so that others may see Jesus Christ through your life. Then make a list of a few people whom you see Christ in, and tell them this week.

Day 5

What Happens to Those Who Stand Against God?

Encounter the Word
Exodus 7:8-24

Explore the Word

Pharaoh is still not convinced or even threatened by God's warning, so the narrative of the plagues begins. God never does anything randomly or by chance. We may never fully understand all His purposes, but it's exciting to discover some of the amazing possibilities, especially in the plagues. The first plague, turning the Nile River into blood, has some interesting ironies. A reason God chose this plague first could have been His desire to discredit the Egyptian god Hapi, which the Nile River represented. In verse 7:15, the phrase "as he goes out to the water" implies that Pharaoh might have been offering a sacrifice or paying homage to Hapi. Another possibility is that this could have been God's payback for Pharaoh's earlier decree to kill off the Hebrew male babies by throwing them into the Nile.

Live the Word

The severity of God's judgment is overwhelming. We can rest in the fact that we are His children, but we can also praise Him for His power and might. Read Psalm 8, and take some time to write your own psalm of praise to Him.

Entering In #3

The Hardening

Contemplation

It's easy to quickly dismiss and overlook the unique and difficult situation Pharaoh is in. Moses had grown up in his household. Now imagine that day when Moses realizes who his real family is and flees Egypt. I'm sure that Pharaoh feels the range of emotions like anger, hurt, sadness, and great loss. Now after years of healing or at least coming to grips with the loss, Moses returns with bad news. The fact that Egypt had a slave labor force was not uncommon in that time, so when Moses demands that Pharaoh release some two million slaves, it's no surprise that his response is a flat "no." Review this section and try to empathize with what Pharaoh was feeling and experiencing.

Communication

We could say that Pharaoh was having one of those moments of divine opportunity that God continued to place before him. It must have been difficult for him as the ruler of a great nation that's being challenged by a criminal shepherd out to destroy his whole economic system. But as we saw in our first encounter, this is no excuse. In fact, excuses are a form of rebellion or disobedience that eventually hardens a heart. Review the reading for the week, and highlight the times where Pharaoh's heart is mentioned.

Community

Hardened hearts don't just happen to those who don't believe. In Mark 6:51-53; 8:16-18; and Hebrews 3:13, we see that we as Christ-followers can have hardened hearts. What causes hardening of a heart? The top two are sin and lack of connection to a body of believers (the Church). When sin begins to take root into a life, a person begins to feel guilt and typically disconnects from the body. When people like this are confronted, they can become defensive and make excuses. Those excuses trap and keep their hearts hardened to the truth. What is your heart's condition like?

Compassion

When others around us have hearts that are hard, Scripture teaches that we're to love them. Love and encouragement touch people as if Jesus himself were there. Out of love, pray and ask the Holy Spirit for those you need to reach out to this week.

Day 1

Frogs, Gnats and Flies

Encounter the Word
Exodus 8:1-32

Explore the Word
Pharaoh is not softening in his position but is hardening his heart. The situation has become very tense. The Nile River has turned to blood and has created a foul stench in the land (except for where the Hebrews live) and has killed the fish and other life in it. This is believed to be the frog's reproductive season, and they are now forced onto the land most likely carrying deadly bacteria and disease. The Egyptians also had another pagan god, Heqt, that was a frog-headed goddess of fertility for Egyptian women in childbirth. Another possible reason for God's use of this plague was to bring payback for Pharaoh's other decree when he asked the midwives to kill the Hebrew baby boys upon delivery. The last observation to note is in verses 18-19, in which Pharaoh's magicians retire when failing to keep up with God's plagues; they say, "This is the finger of God."

Live the Word
Sometimes we can run such a fast-paced lifestyle so full of activity that we forget to stop and recognize "the finger of God." He's at work right now in the world, in your city, and in your life. Do you see it? Take some time to walk, and think about all the ways where God's finger is touching you and those around you. Thank Him for that.

Day 2

Livestock, Boils, and Hail

Encounter the Word

Exodus 9:1-35

Explore the Word

Could you imagine being an Egyptian experiencing a bloody river, an invasion of frogs, swarms of flies, and now the death of all your lifestock? What would make this even more shocking is that your Hebrew slaves and their land of Goshen are not affected by any of it. All of their water is unchanged, no frogs in their part of the land, and all their cattle and animals healthy and even reproducing at an impressive rate. The ultimate insult for the Egyptians is that each of the plagues destroyed their pagan gods and rituals. This would have changed and even broken the hearts of most people—but not Pharaoh. God continues with the plagues of boils and hail, which once again does not harm the Hebrews at all. It is an awesome show of God's power and authority over humanity and its false gods.

Live the Word

Sometimes we can find ourselves in a place where we've developed our own set of gods. These, of course, are not real but have an influence over us and can cause us to feel that they make us powerful. These false gods can be anything that we put before God himself—status, education, wealth, sexual activity, and more. God is a jealous God and will not tolerate false gods in our life. What are those false gods in your life? What do you place before Almighty God? Journal your thoughts, and release them to God.

Day 3

Locusts and Darkness

Encounter the Word
Exodus 10:1-29

Explore the Word
Today a plague of locust would still be regarded as a horrible tragedy and loss. Locusts reproduce in moist and humid environments and can completely destroy a square mile of fields and crops overnight. In the biblical narrative, Pharaoh's officials are convinced and frustrated that their leader is so blind that he cannot see that his kingdom lies in ruin (10:7). God sends the locusts, and nothing green remains in Egypt—but Pharaoh is unchanged in his heart. God's next plague of darkness has some interesting significance in regard to the pagan sun goddess. This act of God leaves Egypt with no other pagan god to call on—they are now godless.

Live the Word
Read through the following verses from Psalms, and incorporate them as your own praises to God: Psalm 40:4; 82:1; 86:8; 95:3; 96:4; 97:7; 97:9; 106:28; 135:5; 136:2.

Day 4

Firstborn

Encounter the Word
Exodus 11:1-10

Explore the Word
In this passage we reach the end of the plagues with one that leaves no room for doubt. In the end of chapter 10, Pharaoh has given a death threat to Moses which provokes the 10th plague. This plague, unlike any of the previous ones, is outside the realm of nature. It cannot be mistaken for a random act of nature; it is not from anything earthly but is an awesome display of God and His power. Reread verses 6-7. You see that God is making His point very clear: these Hebrews are His chosen people, and He will protect them and anything they own.

Live the Word
Being "firstborn" is not regarded today as important and significant as back in biblical times. The firstborn males of a family would receive the birthright from their fathers, which had spiritual and material benefit. Read Romans 8:29. Jesus is the firstborn of God, and we become recipients of that birthright through Jesus Christ. Have you ever just spent time thanking God for that gift? Take time to pray and thank Him for choosing you.

Day 5

The Passover

Encounter the Word
Exodus 12:1-30

Explore the Word
There's something special when we discover the source or beginning of a religious tradition. It brings depth, meaning, and a strong sense of divine purpose for it. Many of our traditions today might seem shallow to you or others, but most come from a strong spiritual beginning in Scripture. This passage marks the beginning of one of those religious traditions called Passover, which we see Jesus himself celebrate before His own death (He is firstborn). The word "Passover" in the original Hebrew language means just that—"to pass over"—and implies that the Hebrews would be "passed over"—spared from death.

Live the Word
On this journey through Exodus you are hopefully gaining a depth and appreciation for the New Testament life of Jesus and birth of the Church. Spend some time journaling your thoughts of what you have learned and how this affects what you know of Jesus Christ and the Church.

Entering In #4

And the Blood Was Spilt

Contemplation

This week we stop to reflect on perhaps one of the most significant and symbolic events in the Old Testament, the Passover. Different denominations debate on exactly when it was, but most recognize it as a key spiritual event to observe. What makes this day so significant is that it would lay the groundwork for Jesus himself to celebrate but also, and more importantly, become the "Lamb" sacrifice whose blood causes death to *pass over*. It's a powerful display of God's divine purpose to know that He designs a spiritual ceremony hundreds of years before His own Son would shed His own blood. God established blood as a covering for sin as far back as Genesis 6:9, and it became a standard religious practice in Leviticus 17:11—"The life of a creature is in the blood, and I have given it to you to make atonement for yourselves on the altar; it is the blood that makes atonement for one's life."

Communication

As Christians we celebrate this spiritually historic event of our own Passover when Jesus died and shed His blood for us on the Cross so that we would be able to live forever with Him. If you simply look at those few days of Easter and assume that's it, you miss out on the weight of the event. It would be like taking a great novel and ripping out the climax to read only that section, throwing away the rest of the story and claiming that you've read the book. You see the story of Scripture from Genesis is a story that brings power to Jesus' life and death and purpose for our lives today. Read the following passages, and meditate on this blood sacrifice established for you.

Matthew 26:27-29
John 6:52-56
Romans 3:21-26
Hebrews 9:11-13
1 Peter 1:18-20

Community

It's important that all of us as Christ followers understand the depth and power of this story. It helps us fully appreciate God's gift to us but also can provide us with a greater urgency to share it with others. Figuratively speaking, we're in a similar place of bondage in this sinful world, and without the blood of the Lamb (Jesus Christ) covering our lives, we'll die!

Compassion

Our understanding of Jesus' sacrifice is remembered in what we call communion. It's a powerful reminder of the cost of our sin and the "Passover" experience that we have claimed—and that we have victory over death forever.

Read 1 Corinthians 11:23-32 and celebrate communion with another Christ follower. (If this is not allowable in your denomination, seek out the leadership of your church to serve you communion as a group.)

Day 1

Free from . . . Free to . . .

Encounter the Word
Read Exodus 12:31-42

Explore the Word
Imagine this: after years of slavery, after weeks of amazing signs from God—the people of God are finally free. Freedom. Freedom from what has bound them. Freedom from fear. Freedom from oppression. Freedom from hard labor. They are now free, not only free *from* things but free *to* some other realities.

They're free to dream. They're free to live. They're free to choose. They're free to celebrate. They're free to be what they have only imagined. They are free because of God. That's why they remember Him and honor Him. Freedom.

Are there things you've been freed from? Are there things you've been freed by God to be and do? Have you remembered those things? Have you thanked Him? Have you honored Him?

Live the Word
Take just a few moments to think about the things you've been freed from in your life. Take a piece of paper and make two columns. In one column write down the things you've been freed from. In the other column write down the things you're free to be and do in Him. Spend a few moments in prayer to thank God for all the things you've been freed from and all the things you've been freed to be and become in Him. You might want to write out your prayer to God as a love letter to Him.

Day 2

All Alone?

Encounter the Word
Read Exodus 12:43-51

Explore the Word
In the middle of the restrictions and guidelines for celebrating the Passover comes the following: "The whole community of Israel must celebrate it" (12:47). What was God trying to communicate to the forthcoming nation of Israel? In a word—*community*.

Being a follower of Jesus is not an individual endeavor—it it's a community movement. We were never meant to be individually independent as followers of God; we were made for community. We need each other. We need to live in community with other believers. There's power in knowing that you're a part of something larger than yourself, that you're a part of a movement.

The Israelites were told to celebrate as a "whole community" so that they would never forget the fact that everyone matters, everyone is needed, and that freedom is for everyone. The whole community was free. The whole community was to celebrate—a community of people experiencing freedom together, honoring the God of their fathers, and finding strength in common.

Live the Word
Think of three people who are in your "community" of people that you are "doing life with" right now. Call them today and thank them for being a part of your life. Share with them what God has been doing in your life as a way of celebrating all that He has done.

Day 3
Why Do You Do the Things You Do?

Encounter the Word
Read Exodus 13:1-16

Explore the Word

Why do we do the things we do? Let's say that I bring home flowers for my wife, Jamie. She's thrilled and looks at me and says, "You didn't need to do that." What if I replied, "Well, that's my duty, isn't it?"? Or what if I said, "I know, Honey—they really weren't that expensive. I just thought you needed them"? How would she feel? She wouldn't even want the flowers, would she?

I wonder if that's how God feels sometimes.

Here I am coming to God with my religious acts, in essence saying, "Well, it's my duty, isn't it?" All the while He's crying out, "I don't want your religious acts if they come from duty—I want your heart." God's desire is that our lives be lived as a response to all that He's done for us, not because we feel that we "need" to. So—duty or response? Why do you do the things you do?

Live the Word
Think through the following questions:

1. Why do you think God wants our heart and not our "duty"? How do you think He feels about our "duty"?

2. What are some things you're doing spiritually purely because of duty?

Take a few moments to pray right now, confessing to God where you've been following Him out of duty. Ask Him to give you a heart that overflows with Him and responds by following Jesus out of love.

Day 4
Have You Forgotten?

Encounter the Word
Read Exodus 13:17—14:31

Explore the Word
Ever notice how short our memory really is? I'm continually blown away by how selective the Israelites' memory really is. No more than two or so short chapters earlier, they're in hard labor, slaving under the oppression of the Egyptians. They cry out to God for deliverance, and He acts. They're free. Yet here they are, a handful of chapters later, facing the Red Sea and the Egyptian army, and somehow God isn't looking so faithful, and Egypt is looking better and better. Really? Seems that they've forgotten something (or Someone).

Yet I can't be too critical, because I do the same thing, maybe even worse. I'm sometimes sickened by my own short-term memory when it comes to the faithfulness of God in my life. Time and time again, He has faithfully moved in my life, acting in ways that I could never have imagined. Yet encounter another tough time, and my attitude can easily be *Where are you, God? You know, God, sometimes I think I'd be better off . . .* Really?

It often seems I've forgotten something (or Someone) as well.

Live the Word
Take a piece of paper and try to write down for the next week all the ways in which God shows His faithfulness to you. At the end of the week, review your list, thanking Him for all He is and does in your life.

Day 5

A Moment in Time

Encounter the Word
Read Exodus 15:1-27

Explore the Word
Through the ages people have used songs and poetry to capture the passion of their heart in worship and praise of God. What's amazing is that they've been written down for future generations to catch a glimpse into the story of what God was doing in their lives. The Scriptures are the story of God's activity in our world and in the lives of people.

In today's reading, Moses writes a song of praise to God, capturing the emotion and passion of the Red Sea experience. It's his cry of praise and worship of God, written down so that you can enter into the celebration of what God did in the midst of the nation of Israel thousands of years ago.

What about you? Anything worth worshiping God over?

Live the Word
Take a few minutes to craft your own song or poetic response to what God has been doing in your life. Who knows? Maybe your words will encourage the faith journey of someone else.

"Who among the gods is like you, O LORD? Who is like you?" _____

_____

_____

_____.

What's Your Red Sea Moment?

Contemplation

Exodus was a sacred journey for the nation of Israel. God was calling the Israelites into a dependant relationship with Him, one that would solidify their identity as His people. One of those hard lessons, forged in the crucible of reality, was that God, Yahweh, was the ever-present God, living and active. He had (and still does have) the ability to step into our present-day life with power, saying, "I am here." And that's exactly what He did at the Red Sea in Exodus 14, and it left an indelible mark.

God leads the nation of Israel to the edge of the Red Sea while the elite army of Egypt is in hot pursuit. Once at the Red Sea, the Israelites awaken to the reality of the situation: on one side an impossible body of water to cross, on the other side Pharaoh's troops bearing down on them. Scared, they do the only thing they can do: cry out to God.

Ever been in that place? The place where there's no conceivable way out and no conceivable answer? Ever been in a situation in which your only option was to cry out to the living God, saying, *There's nothing I can do here, God. If You don't show up, I'm done here.* Remember how boldly the Israelites marched out of Egypt? Now look at them. They had seen the amazing hand of God on their behalf. Now what? How short our memories truly are! When life was easy, it was easy to follow God—but now, when the times are tough? Sounds a lot like us today.

The Israelites cry out to God, and Moses answers for God: "Do not be afraid. Stand firm and you will see the deliverance the LORD will bring today. . . . you need only be still" (Exodus 14:13-14). Not exactly comforting: "I know you're facing a seemingly impossible situation, so here's what we're gonna do—stand there and do nothing!" In our economy it's insane, but in God's it's pure wisdom.

In essence God is saying, *Let go. Stand back. Only be still.* We, like the Israelites, have nothing to offer the situation. We have nothing in and of ourselves that helps ourselves, and that's the plan. It's all about God and who He is and what He can do on our behalf. All this is done through Him and for His glory, so that we can do nothing else but stand back and be amazed at our God!

You know the rest of their story. The waters part. The people walk through on dry land. The Egyptian army is swept away. God shows up, for His glory.

But what about you and your story? Where do you need God to show up? What's your Red Sea moment? Where are you crying out to God, *There's nothing I can do here, God. If You don't show up, I'm done here.* All of us have these opportune times. They're God-ordained moments in which He wants to do something remarkable in our lives, something only He can do, to let us know *I am here.*

Communication

Read Psalm 46:10 and reflect on those words. What do they mean for you today? What's your Red Sea moment? Take a piece of paper and write out the words to Psalm

46:10 on the top, and then underneath describe your Red Sea moment. Be as honest and straightforward as possible. Don't hold anything back. Share this with your small group.

Community

While at your group, share your heart and thoughts on the crossing of the Red Sea. Share your Red Sea moment. Pray for each other and each other's Red Sea moment. As an act of trust in the ever-present God, as a group, craft a prayer for the bottom of your piece of paper. Have everyone write the prayer out on the bottom of the sheet. Place the piece of paper in your Bible at Exodus 14. Keep praying. Keep trusting. He will show up for your Red Sea moment.

Day 1

Don't Live off Yesterday

Encounter the Word

Read Exodus 16:1-36

Explore the Word

Isn't it amazing that only one chapter earlier, Moses and the Israelites are singing praises to God for His faithfulness, and here we are in chapter 16 and "the whole community" was grumbling against Moses and Aaron? So much for remembering the awesome power and faithfulness of God!

He hears their cries and brings forth manna for them to eat. Moses tells his people to take only enough for the day and not to keep any of it until morning.

Strange instructions? Perhaps, but God is trying to make a point with the nation. "Take only enough for the day. I want you to trust me daily. I want you to come back tomorrow seeking and being dependent on me." Isn't it funny how we can so easily live off what God has done in the past? We look back and remember the faithfulness of God long past, but what about today? Where is He moving today? More importantly, are you "seeking and being dependent" upon Him? God doesn't want us living off yesterday's manna. He wants us to be seeking Him afresh every day, eyes wide open to the ever-present activity of God going on all around us.

Are you living off yesterday's manna? You know how well that worked out for the Israelites, right?

Live the Word

"Where is God moving in your life today?" That's a great question! End your time with God today by asking Him to open your eyes today to people and situations in which He is moving in all around you. At the end of the day, take stock of what you saw and heard. Write down your insights of the day. Where was God today? What was He up to in the lives of others? What was He up to in your life?

Day 2

Do You Trust Him?

Encounter the Word
Read Exodus 17:1-7

Explore the Word
Ever notice that at the heart of a grumbling spirit is a spirit of self-centeredness? We grumble because we're focusing on ourselves and our situation. Our situation is not going as we would like it to, so we let everyone, including God, hear about it! But it doesn't stop there.

At the true heart of self-centeredness is a lack of trust. We focus on ourselves, because we truly don't believe that anyone else will look after our interests, including God. We subtly believe that He will not truly take care of us, so we think we need to take action on our own.

The Israelites grumbled because they lacked trust, trust that God would provide, even though they had seen Him meet their needs time and time again. We see that—how come *they* don't? We can easily point out time and again that God was faithful: the departure from Egypt, the parting of the Red Sea, the manna, and so on. "Why can't they see and trust God?" we say.

Interesting how we can be so blind as well.

Live the Word
What are some areas of your life where you're feeling disappointed or let down by God? Go back and read the paper you have in your Bible at Exodus 14. Read the prayer. Has He been faithful? Get a concordance and find five verses that speak of God's faithfulness and trustworthiness. Pick one of those verses and memorize it for your next small group meeting.

Day 3
Allowing Others Inside

Encounter the Word
Read Exodus 17:8-16

Explore the Word
Here we find Moses standing on the hillside, overlooking the battle between the Israelites and the Amalekites at a place called Rephidim. The Scriptures tell us an amazing story. "As long as Moses held up his hands, the Israelites were winning, but whenever he lowered his hands, the Amalekites were winning." As the battle rages, Moses tires. His hands drop. The Amalekites are winning. It is then that Aaron and Hur teach Moses a lesson he will not soon forget—we need each other.

They take Moses, set him on a rock, and hold his hands up for him. The Amalekites are defeated.

In our own strength, we can do little. We can operate under our own strength for a little while, but not long enough. We need each other. We need "community." We need to allow others to help.

Sometimes allowing others to help can be tough. We want to be able to do it on our own, but that's not how it works. We were never meant to travel the journey of being a follower of Jesus alone. We were built for community. We need each other.

Live the Word
Remember the three people you called earlier to celebrate all that God was doing in your life? Now comes the hard part. Call them back today and share what God is doing, but this time share with them one thing they can do to help you in your faith journey. Be bold. Be honest.

Day 4

A Word of Advice

Encounter the Word
Read Exodus 18:1-27

Explore the Word

Sometimes we're so busy that we often lose focus on the larger reality of our lives. It's in those times that God often brings someone to speak truth into our lives. As with a mirror held to our faces, we see the truth.

Today we find Moses entertaining his father-in-law, Jethro, who has come to visit his son-in-law. After a night of celebrating all that God has done for the nation, Moses goes out to serve as judge for all the people.

Jethro sees the line of people. He hears their deep sighs as they wait. He thinks, *This is not right. There must be a better way.* He steps in and mirror-like says, "The work is too heavy for you; you cannot handle it alone" (Exodus 18:18). His advice? Find out what you're good at, and do it. Don't try to be all things to all people, because the job is too heavy for you.

God has gifted each of us in various ways. Working together, we can accomplish all that God has in mind for us, but once again, it's not about one person doing the entire job. Find what you're good at, and do it with all your might! Don't try to be everything; rest in who God has made you to be.

Live the Word
Find someone you trust, and ask him or her the following questions:

1. What am I really good at?

2. What am I truly gifted in?

3. How can I be used in that area?

Day 5

A Sacred Purpose

Encounter the Word
Read Exodus 19:1-25

Explore the Word

Consecration. Literally it means to "set aside or devote something or someone for a sacred purpose." That's such a great picture of what's going in today's Scripture reading. God is calling Moses to "consecrate" the people, to make them ready for the visitation of the presence of God, because He has a purpose in mind—He wants to enter into the covenant with His people.

The covenant is God's agreement with the people of how they should live in relationship with Him. It was an opportunity for them to live as God's chosen people, not an obligation to carry out a set of rules. But in order to enter into the covenant and be in the presence of God, they had to consecrate themselves.

As you look at your life today, are there any areas you need to consecrate? Are there areas that you know God is not in control of? Are there any areas of sin, which, of course, simply can't be in the presence of a holy God? Like the Israelites, God is calling you to "consecrate" yourself for the holy task of knowing and following Him in covenant.

Live the Word

Take a few moments to reflect on the word "consecrate." Get a concordance, or look in the back of your Bible for all the places the word "consecrate" occurs throughout Scripture. Read a few of the passages where the word is used, then write a definition. Pray about your own consecration to the Lord, giving Him those areas that need to be consecrated.

Entering In #6

The Desert and a New Identity

Contemplation

The desert is a crucible that shows the true state of your heart. For the Israelites, the desert is a place where they leave behind their identity as slaves and are given a new vision of who they are and who they will become. The desert is a land of paradox. Though desolate, the desert is the very place they find themselves. Although demanding, it builds character. Although destructive, it builds deeper bonds of connection. Although terribly isolating, it builds community. The desert is God's chosen tool to build a nation, a people for himself.

In Exodus 19 Moses climbs Mount Sinai to meet with God. He goes up the leader of a people and comes down the leader of a nation. While on the top the mountain, Moses speaks with God. God reminds the people through Moses of all He has done for them (vv. 3-4). He calls them into covenant with himself, offering them three unique blessings, that they would be (1) a treasured possession, (2) a kingdom of priests, and (3) a holy nation.

Treasured Possession. God calls Israel "a treasured possession," signifying that the people would be God's valuable property and distinct treasure, set aside for a marked purpose. In saying this, God was communicating that they were intensely valuable to Him. The community was a treasure that God saw enormous value in.

A Kingdom of Priests. Although there was a specific office of "priest," God was placing on every member of the community the responsibility of being a priest to others, to care for and be the spiritual representation of the kingdom of God. Everyone regardless of position, standing, or even spiritual stature had a responsibility in this new community to play a role in caring for each other and sharing the burden of helping others see God and live in covenant with Him.

A Holy Nation. The Israelites were to be a nation that was holy, not because of doing the right things but because of their association with a holy God. They were holy because God was in their midst. His holiness changed them and made them holy.

As it was with the Israelites, so it is with us. When we enter into covenant with God, through the death and resurrection of Jesus Christ, we're changed. We're no longer the same. We're His treasured possession, set aside for a marked purpose—to carry His love and redemption to a lost and dying world. We walk through this world as priests, spiritually crying out and mediating between God and humanity, on behalf of those God places in our lives. We're a "holy gathering" of followers, taking His holiness as an aroma with us into the world, where we act as a kingdom of priests.

Communication

The language of Exodus 19 is not the only place that God speaks of His followers in such a way. Read the following passages, writing down all the images that are used of God's people. As a small group, discuss what some of these mean and how they apply to your lives as followers of God.

Ezekiel 11:19-20
2 Corinthians 2:14-17
2 Corinthians 5:17-21
Ephesians 2:8-10
1 Peter 2:9-11

Community

Realizing that you're a "holy gathering" as a small group, take a few moments in your small group time to "commission" one another. Select one person, and place him or her in the middle of the group. As a group, pray a blessing upon the person, "commissioning" him or her to go forth from your group to be a treasured possession, a priest of the Kingdom, and a member of a "holy gathering." Do this for each person in your group.

Day 1

Are These Words for Me?

Encounter the Word
Exodus 20:1-26

Explore the Word
The Ten Commandments are very significant and reappear throughout portions of the Bible. The original Hebrew translation is actually "the Ten Words." The tablets were written fully on each of the tablets so that one could be placed into the Ark of the covenant and the other kept for the people. God says in 19:5, "If you obey me fully . . . you will be my treasured possession." This becomes a binding contract between God and the Israelites. Can you imagine what it must have felt like to have Moses come down from Mount Sinai and say, "God has spoken 10 words for us to live by"? After all that has transpired in this story for the Israelites, you know they were anxiously waiting to hear them.

Live the Word
As you read through the "Ten Words," take some time to reflect on whether they're a guide for you today. Why? Which ones have you broken? How do these Words bring order to our world today?

Day 2

How Am I to Treat Others?

Encounter the Word

Exodus 21:1-36

Explore the Word

Some portions of Scripture don't get enough credit for their significance in the whole Story of God redeeming a lost people. These following passages of God's rules and regulations represent much more than rules—they're known as the Book of the Covenant, which are full of ethical, social, moral, civil, and criminal guides that are still used today. Take some time to reread this section, remembering the context and time back then. The Israelites, over two million strong, are in a desert, hearing God's way for them to live with Him and each other.

Live the Word

As you read this section, what's different about how God views slaves and servants? What values do you see being established in these verses? Read Galatians 4:6-7. What new appreciation do you have for this passage? What other verses in the Bible speak to how we should treat others? (A next step would be to look up all the verses in the New Testament dealing with slavery and observe the impact of using the metaphor of being slaves.)

Day 3

Is This All Mine?

Encounter the Word

Exodus 22:1-31

Explore the Word

Food, clothing, water and livestock were of high value to the people of this time in history. It should be of no surprise to us that given the population of this people, crime and disputes would arise often. God establishes His Word on how to deal with both our property and the property of others. Again, take some time to reread this section, thinking about what it might have felt like hearing these for the first time.

Live the Word

As you read this section, what's different about how God views property? What values do you see being established in these verses? What do you own? Who gave it to you? Now look up on your own any New Testament passage dealing with property, and observe the impact of this subject.

Day 4

A Jealous God

Encounter the Word

Exodus 23:1-19

Explore the Word

Today's reading is the continuation of God's design for living together with people and himself. Focus on verse 14: "Three times a year you are to celebrate a festival to me." Does this sound awkward—that God would set up parties in His own honor? There was no question for the Israelites with these festivals; they are still recognized today in some religious denominations. They understood something about God because of their firsthand journey with Him, which we can miss because of our distance from those events. Read Exodus 20:4-6. What character trait does God reveal of himself?

Live the Word

We don't really see jealousy as something of a good character trait today, but make no mistake—God is a jealous God who desires your full worship. Is your life His alone? Meditate and ask the Holy Spirit to identify those areas that are not fully His, and surrender them to Him.

Day 5

The Blessings of God

Encounter the Word

Exodus 23:20-33

Explore the Word

Angels are one of those mysterious beings of God and His kingdom that will never be fully understood until we're in heaven. What we do know is that angels play significant roles throughout Scripture. They're primarily God's messengers to humanity and are at His service. We're not to worship them but see them as ambassadors of God to us. In today's reading, focus on verses 25-26 and notice this amazing promise God gives that His angel will carry out. The Israelites, over two million in number, are in a desert, with no electricity, hospitals, or grocery stores—do you get the picture? God's blessing would be on their food and water supplies, health, children, and even their lifespan. This would be an amazing promise for even today, but to have this blessing back then must have been great news.

Live the Word

What news of blessing has God brought to your life? It might not have been an angel bringing that message, but what other ways has God shown you His blessings for you and your life? Take some time to reflect with a few friends about the blessings in your life.

Obligation or Opportunity?

Contemplation

This week's encounter with the Word has been primarily about God's establishing the way He wants His people to live together, work together, and worship together. I know many of us can quickly categorize these "ways" as rules. They're commandments that God said they must obey. We never really like rules or hearing a commandment, do we? It's easy to assume that this is how the Israelites felt and thought. Let me challenge that assumption. Read Exodus 19:7-8. Moses is meeting with God, and God tells Moses that He will bless the people if they will obey what He asks. What do the elders of the people respond together saying? "We will do everything the LORD has said." Have the Ten Commandments been given yet? No, the Israelites don't even know what God is going to ask of them, but they don't care—they'll do everything! The question is, "Why?"

Communication

When we have guidelines or rules in our life, we can look at them in one of two ways. We can see them as a weighty obligation or duty that we dread, or we can see them as an opportunity to be under the blessing of God. Think about getting a driver's license. You have or will have to take a test about the rules and are expected to obey them throughout your entire driving life. You could see this as a bummer since it doesn't allow you to make your own decisions about how you want to drive and creates a dreadful obligation. Or you see this amazing privilege and opportunity to travel the network of roads quickly and have a level of safety, which provides freedom. I believe the Israelites viewed the guidelines for living as an opportunity to live underneath the blessing of God. They felt honored and blessed to have God speak "words" to them to live by.

Compassion

What word best describes your spiritual life? Is it an obligation that's heavy and full of guilt, or is it an opportunity to be underneath God's hand of blessing and protection? List all the areas in your spiritual life that you feel obligated to obey. Read Proverbs 4:3-5, and ask God to give you an attitude that views His Word as an opportunity for life.

Day 1

Being a True Christ Follower

Encounter the Word

Read Exodus 24:1-18

Explore the Word

Obedience. What God is looking for today is people who will stand and say, *Yes, God. I'll do what you say. I'm willing to follow you.*

But that's easier said than done. We live in a society where good intentions are good enough. For far too many people, following Jesus is all about believing the right thing but not necessarily having that change the way we live. We want to be "Christ followers," but tragically, our lives look little different than the world around us. Following Christ is marked by obedience.

Jesus had something to say about being a true follower. "Why do you call me, 'Lord, Lord,' and do not do what I say?" (Luke 6:46) Why is it that there are so many people who claim to follow Christ but are not willing to be obedient to His words? If you and I are followers of Jesus, our lives will be marked by obedience to the things He said we should do.

How about you? Are you willing?

Live the Word

Take a courageous step today. Call someone in your small group who knows you very well, and ask him or her this question: "Does my life match up to being an obedient follower of Jesus?" Listen carefully. Be open to what God may be saying through that person.

Day 2

Being a Part of the Plan

Encounter the Word
Read Exodus 25:1-9

Explore the Word
At this point in the journey of Israel, God is about to give the Israelites the instructions for building the Tabernacle, the place where God's presence will be made manifest among them as they travel. To begin this process, God calls Moses to send a message to Israel: "Those whose hearts are moved, give to this work."

Giving is not just for the gift given—it's also to impact the heart of the giver. God wants to teach us a lesson about giving as we give to others. What we have is truly not our own but is to be seen as resources to meet the needs of others.

The items that the nation gives are items they have carried with them since leaving Egypt. Not knowing why they would need the items they're carrying, the Israelites are now shown a greater truth—God has a plan, and our giving is a part of that plan. God is looking for people whose hearts are moved to give. He's looking for people who are willing to give, not "reluctantly or under compulsion" (2 Corinthians 9:7), but see their giving as a part of God's ultimate plan. Is that you?

Live the Word
Take a few moments and ask God to open your eyes to the needs around you and how your giving may be a part of His plan. Find one thing today that you can physically give to, whether it's your time, your talent, or your treasure.

Day 3

His Word Is Life

Encounter the Word
Read Exodus 25:10-40

Explore the Word
The instruction for building the Tabernacle and the items inside were given to Moses from the inside outward, and from the most important, or most holy, to the least. In the center of the Tabernacle was the most holy place, called "the holy of holies." In it was the most important item— the ark of the covenant.

The ark was a box made of acacia wood, overlaid with gold, with the lid made of solid gold. But gold was not the most important feature. It was what was inside—the "Testimony," or the tablet with the "Ten Words" on it. In Middle East culture, the most holy place in a temple of worship was the inner sanctum, which usually held a box or altar that contained the most important artifact of that particular religion, the carved image of that god. Isn't it interesting that in the ark of the God of Israel is the most important artifact of the relationship God had with the nation—not His image, but His written covenant? The words of God are to be valued and taken seriously. The Bible, God's written Word, is our doorway into the heart of God. We read it and we follow it, to be able to know God and live in a right relationship with Him.

Live the Word
Read Psalm 119:9-16, and reflect on the words written there. Take a piece of paper and rewrite that portion of the Psalm in your own words as a prayer to God.

Day 4

Behind the Curtain

Encounter the Word

Read Exodus 26:1-36

Explore the Word

If you think about it, curtains are usually meant to hide something. There's a mystery to things that are behind curtains.

The Tabernacle was made from a series of curtains, but none more important than the curtain between the "holy place" and the "holy of holies." It was this curtain that was always kept drawn, separating God from the people. Behind the curtain was the presence of God, His written covenant with the people, and the ark.

Hidden. Separate. Different. Mysterious.

Ever wonder what the Israelites thought about when they considered what was behind the curtain? Were they drawn to it?

There's something mysterious about God. We can never fully grasp all that He is and His ways. We catch glimpses of Him in the pages of the Scriptures, but there still seems so much about Him that's mysterious. I think He planned it that way so we would seek Him and so that He would have the joy of revealing himself more fully to us.

Hidden. Separate. Different. Mysterious.

Awakened! Revealed! Discovery!

Live the Word

If you could ask God one question, knowing you would get an answer, what would it be? Take the next few minutes to talk to God about that area. Ask for insight where you need it. Ask Him to reveal himself more fully and deeply to you. Ask Him to give you a glimpse behind the curtain, that you would know Him more fully.

Day 5

The Image of the Altar

Encounter the Word
Read Exodus 27:1-21

Explore the Word

It's been said that a picture is worth a thousand words. This is no truer than in Eastern cultures. We often approach our Christianity and truth through a Western mind-set—one built on words and logic. Yet the Eastern mindset grasped truth in a very different way—through images.

Images capture truth. Images help us reflect on the deeper parts of God and His character. In the Tabernacle was an image that almost every Israelite knew. It was an image they lived with every day—the image of the altar.

The altar was in the outer court and was the only part of the Tabernacle that was accessible to anyone over the age of 12. It was on this altar that the offerings were made. Imagine being 12 years old and going to the Tabernacle with your father and seeing an animal sacrifice for the first time. Think of the power of that image.

"Daddy, why is the priest doing that?"

"For you."

"For me? Why, Daddy?"

"Because you need forgiveness."

"I do?"

"Yes, we all do—that's why we do this. The animal is killed in our place. Its blood is spilled in place of ours. It pays the price, and we go free."

"Daddy, why is that man hanging on the Cross?"

Live the Word

Write a letter to God, thanking Him for the Cross—the image of your salvation.

Entering In #8

Life Behind the Curtain

Contemplation

While in the desert, the nation of Israel is given the awesome task of building the Tabernacle, a physical place for the presence of God to make himself manifest—a portable sanctuary. God, the eternal Creator of the universe, will dwell among His people Israel.

The Physical Construction

The Tabernacle was 100 cubits long by 50 cubits wide, with an entrance of 20 cubits on one side. A cubit was anywhere from 17 to 20 inches in length. It was divided up into three main sections—the outer court (which expanded all around the inside of the Tabernacle, excluding a tent in the middle where the two other sections were), the holy place, and the holy of holies. The outer court was available for the community to enter. The holy place was accessible only to the priests, while the holy of holies was accessible only to the high priest, and only once a year in order to come before the Lord.

In the outer court were two objects—an altar for burnt offerings, and a washbasin. The altar was where the priest would offer the sacrifices for the people. Every morning and evening a lamb was sacrificed on the altar. The washbasin was used for the priest to ceremonially wash his hands and feet before entering the holy place or performing any sacred ritual.

The holy place was the outer section of a tent-like building in the middle of the Tabernacle and was two-thirds of this inner tent structure. It had a curtain entrance. Inside the holy place were three items. First was a table on which 12 loaves of freshly baked bread were placed every Sabbath, arranged in two rows of six loaves. Each loaf represented a tribe of the nation of Israel. The second item was a lamp stand, or menorah, which was lit at dusk and kept burning all night long. The third item was an altar of incense, on which the priest would burn aromatic incense every morning and at twilight.

The most holy section of the Tabernacle was the last third of this inner tent structure, called the holy of holies. It was in here that the ark resided. The ark was a box of acacia wood, overlaid with gold inside and out, with a solid gold lid. On the lid were two cherubim made of pure gold. Inside the ark were the two tablets with the Ten Commandments, or Ten Words, on them. The holy of holies was separated from the holy place by a curtain.

Although portable and made of items the nation took with them out of Egypt, the significance of the Tabernacle was so much more than in the physical construction. A deeply spiritual connection was taking place.

The Spiritual Connection

The Tabernacle was a spiritual extension of the Mt. Sinai experience. It was a physical reminder of what happened on the top of Mt. Sinai. The outer court represented the foot of Mt. Sinai, where the people were allowed to gather and an altar was built. The holy place, where only the priests could go, represented higher up on Mt. Sinai, where only the priests and elders of Israel were allowed to go. The holy of holies, the most holy place, where only one man was allowed to go, corresponded to the top of Mt. Sinai, where only Moses was allowed to come before the Lord.

It is in this place, the cloud-covered top of Mt. Sinai, that God descends in a pillar of fire and gives Moses the written word of the covenant—the very same written covenant that's housed in the ark in the holy of holies. Ironically, when the Tabernacle is completed and God's presence comes to dwell in the holy of holies, He comes in a cloud covering and with a pillar of fire. The Tabernacle is a physical reminder of the covenant and the Mt. Sinai experience—a living sanctuary, corresponding to Mt. Sinai and inhabited by the manifest presence of God.

The Opening

What does all this have to do with us, as followers of Jesus? Everything. By Jesus' day, the Tabernacle was gone, but in its place was the Temple, a non-portable version of the Tabernacle, holding the same spiritual significance. When Jesus hung on the Cross, the curtain in the holy of holies of the Temple was torn in two (Mark 15:33-39), allowing free access to all, not just to a high priest once a year. We now have freedom to commune with God. We have freedom through Christ to a new covenant purchased with His blood!

Communication

Read Mark 15:33-39 and Hebrews 10:19-25. Take some time to reflect on what Jesus has done for you. Journal your thoughts and feelings, and be ready to share them with the group when you meet next.

Community

Before coming to your group, assign someone to find a drawing and a description of the Tabernacle and bring it to the group. Read through the description while looking at the drawing. Read through Mark 15:33-39 and Hebrews 10:19-25 as a group. Share what you wrote as your thoughts and feelings.

Day 1

A Life Set Apart

Encounter the Word
Exodus 28:1-43

Explore the Word
God has been setting up in detail the ways in which the Israelites are to live with each other and with God himself. Once again, God brings instruction concerning the priests who will intercede for the people and perform the priestly duties. Garments are another important distinction for God to establish with those who are set apart. You see this metaphor of garments and priests also throughout the New Testament. It's said that this process of robing these priests took about seven days, which included washing their bodies, robing, and anointing. Priests did not wear shoes, because the grounds of the Temple were holy ground. There's so much to learn in the roles and activities of the priests, but one observation to focus on was that God desired the priests to be set apart for the work of sacrifice and intercession for the people.

Live the Word
We're to be a people who are set apart not from earthly garments but by spiritual ones. Is your life set apart from the world? Read 1 Peter 2:9-12, and take some time to identify any sin that might be hiding your real identity in Christ.

Day 2

The Consecration

Encounter the Word
Exodus 29:1-46

Explore the Word

This is a big chapter that's full of ceremonial procedures for consecrating the priests (Levites). Consecration was simply devoting or setting apart of anything to the worship or service of God. The ceremony of consecration did not actually make things holy or pure but was a dedication solely to God, intending it to be pure. Throughout the scriptures you'll find the act of consecration, like the blood line of Abraham and the tribe of Levi, was both consecrated back in Exodus 13:2, 12, 15. The Hebrews, or Israelites, devoted their fields and cattle, and sometimes the spoils of war, to the Lord (Leviticus 27:28-29). According to the Mosaic Law, the firstborn both of man and beast were consecrated to God.

Live the Word

We learned from yesterday's passage of Scripture that we're to be set apart for God. That means we're different than those who are not—but it also emphasizes the undivided loyalty of our lives. All Christ followers are regarded as consecrated to the Lord (1 Peter 2:9). But sometimes our hearts are divided and not solely His. Read Psalm 86:10-12, and reflect on the areas that are distracting your heart from being fully His.

Day 3

Incense and the Aroma of God

Encounter the Word

Exodus 30:1-21

Explore the Word

In the last few chapters we've learned that God cares a great deal about these priest and what they do—so much that He tells them what to wear, what to do, and what the place should smell like. Today incense has many purposes, such as covering up a bad smell, creating a scent that one likes, or positively affecting one's body or moods. God had instructed its use, among other purposes, to cover the burning flesh smell, to symbolize prayer, and to be offered on Atonement Day. Some scholars believe that it was a way to cloud God's presence from the priest so he would not die.

Live the Word

Read 2 Corinthians 2:14-16. Our lives are to be a sweet-smelling aroma to God. Are you living a life that's a pleasing aroma to God? Burn a candle or incense, and spent some time in prayer, offering your life to be to God what your sense of smell is experiencing—a sweet aroma to God.

Day 4

Anointed for God

Encounter the Word
Exodus 30:22-38

Explore the Word
Anointing was a common practice in biblical culture. It was used for anointing a body, guests, the sick, the dead, and was even a symbol of Jesus' love. Oil in this passage of Scripture has the purpose of setting apart objects and people for divine service. All the Levite priests had to be anointed, as were many of the prophets and kings. The most significant anointing in Scripture is that of the High Priest, Jesus Christ, who was anointed by God for divine service and later as the perfect unblemished sacrifice.

Live the Word
Jesus was and still is the Anointed One. The New Testament language has a greater depth when we can understand some of the Old Testament background. Take out a journal and describe the impact of the following New Testament passages now that you understand anointing a little better:
Acts 4:25-26
2 Corinthians 1:20-22
1 John 2:19-21
1 John 2:26-27

Day 5

Gifted for God

Encounter the Word
Exodus 31:1-18

Explore the Word

Working with our hands and building something brings a great sense of accomplishment and satisfaction. In today's passage we see the beginning of the Temple being built. We might assume that the Israelites just found the construction crews and put them to work, but that was not the case. We see that God himself fills these men with His Spirit, giving them special skills and abilities that were beyond themselves. That had to be an amazing project to watch as it unfolded. Could you imagine being one of those Israelites who couldn't build anything—all of a sudden being filled to carve wooden sculptures, develop plans, and so on? God himself is the designer and project manager, who did not hire the workers but created and gave them the abilities with which to complete the project.

Live the Word

What is so powerful and exciting is that God is still pouring His Spirit into those who receive Jesus as Lord and Savior. And yes, He's still giving special skills, abilities, and talents, called spiritual gifts. Read 1 Corinthians 12 and begin to identify what gifts you believe God has given you.

Entering In #9

The Sabbath: a Sacred Rhythm

Contemplation

Sabbath. Of all the ancient spiritual practices of the Israelites, Sabbath is perhaps the cornerstone. For the Israelites, Sabbath was a sacred rhythm in which one could fully rest and reconnect. It was an opportunity to encounter God with freshness and vitality, not an obligation to be kept. Sabbath is a day that we choose to rest from our own work and remember who God is and recognize what He has provided for us.

Communication

The following is a guide designed to help you experiment with celebrating the Sabbath. Select a day as a group in which you all will celebrate the Sabbath, exploring more deeply this fourth of the "Ten Words" (the Ten Commandments). As with any spiritual practice, one guideline to remember is that we're not trying to add a "religious activity" but are trying to express the freedom we have to connect more deeply with God. After celebrating the Sabbath individually, come together and share any thoughts, feelings, or impressions you may have had during your day of sacred rest.

A Sacred Rhythm

First, begin your Sabbath by waking up without an alarm clock. Let your body tell you when you're ready for the day. Then give your first thoughts and words to God by taking a walk, journaling, or finding a quiet place. Nature is a great place to do this, because it cries out praise to its Creator; it isn't something that humanity can produce.

Second, recognize the relationships in your life that are given to you by God. Have a meal together, and talk about God. You might ask each other to share about personal experiences with Him during the week or take time to discuss an attribute of God. If you have younger siblings, this would be a great time to teach and pass on to them your knowledge and experience of Him.

Third, take a day to enjoy activities and people by being fully present. Free yourself mentally of any "to do's" or feelings of guilt for lack of accomplishments by resting in who God has made you and others around you to be, not for what you do. Suggestions—study or read books that grow your mind concerning God; interact with nature; enjoy being outdoors with others. These are just a few of the ways to practice a Sabbath rhythm. Try not to engage in activities such as television, movies, or video games that unplug you from reality. You want to experience the fullness of reality in Him.

Last, pray whenever and as often as it may come to your mind. Stay in a place of connection with God through the gift of prayer and conversation with Him. You might want to set aside a time during the day to focus on requests that have been on your mind.

Enjoy. Be full of God. Sense Him. Experience Him.

Day 1

The God of Your Mind

Encounter the Word
Read Exodus 32:1-18

Explore the Word

Idolatry. All too often when we think of the word, we see images of people bowing down to an image of a god—a piece of wood, stone, or gold. But idolatry is far more subtle than that.

Idolatry is bowing down to anything except the God revealed in Scripture, and that would include the "image" that we make Him out to be. If we worship anything but the fullness of God revealed in Scripture, we're worshiping an idol.

What's your image of God? Is He the kind grandfather in the sky, looking down ready to give you whatever you want? Is He like a vending machine in the sky—you do your part (i.e. spiritual stuff), and then He needs to do His part (whatever we need Him to do)? Is He a God of love but not a God of wrath?

"These are your gods [idols], O Israel."

What are yours?

Live the Word

Read Isaiah 44:6-20 slowly. Reflect on how you may be worshipping an "idol" of God. Spend your remaining time with God in confession. Confess to Him the ways in which you've made Him an idol, making Him less than He really is. Ask Him to reveal himself more fully to you. Ask Him to expose the wrong assumptions and images you have of Him. Ask Him to open your eyes to all that He is.

Day 2

Honesty

Encounter the Word

Read Exodus 32:19-33:6

Explore the Word

We'll say just about anything to justify ourselves, won't we? Reread verses 21-24, and then compare them to verses 1-6. Notice anything different?

When Moses confronts Aaron, Aaron's story is different than what really happened. He leaves out a few crucial details, namely his responsibility in the idolatry of the nation. We're quick to see his fatal flaw, but what about our own? We, too, have become masters at shifting the blame, trying to make ourselves out to be the innocent ones. We go to great lengths to make ourselves seem like the victims, while all the while God sees and knows the truth.

Psalm 51:6 states, "Surely you desire truth in the inner parts." God desires that at our core we be people who are honest, willing to be transparent with our sin, and owning our own faults. Rather than our trying to hide our sin, God's desire is that we expose it, bring it out into the open, and call it what it is—sin.

Who are we really fooling? Simple—ourselves.

Live the Word

Read James 5:16. This perhaps will be one of the hardest phone calls you'll ever make. Call someone in your small group and be honest with him or her, confessing any area of sin to them you might be guilty of. Ask for the person's help in being honest about your sin in the future. Ask him or her to pray for you.

Day 3

Face to Face

Encounter the Word
Read Exodus 33:7-23

Explore the Word
I wonder what it was like for Moses to speak face to face with God. Think of it. He talked with God "as a man speaks with his friend." Amazing! Moses felt the freedom to speak with God and share what was on his heart. He felt the freedom to be honest with God.

Hebrews 4:13 reminds us that "Nothing in all creation is hidden from God's sight. Everything is uncovered and laid bare before the eyes of him to whom we must give account."

How is it that we can feel the freedom to be honest with God? It's because He sees everything. There's nothing in your life or mine that's hidden from Him. He sees everything—every word, every thought, every motive, every action.

God sees and knows. Nothing in our lives catches Him unaware. We can hide nothing. This could cause us to squirm a little, yet there's another side to it.

Just as God knows us, so He knows all that's going on—our struggles, our hurts, our secret pain. He sees and knows. He understands.

Live the Word
Try an experiment today. Commit to talking to God near every meal (this just gives you a scheduled time). While talking with God, share with Him what's on your heart and mind. Share with Him what you're thinking and

feeling about the day, about what happened the last few hours, or what's coming up in the next few hours. Pray for the people you've seen in the past few hours and for the people you will see. Pray in the present, not for the far-off future. Connect with God over the now, the present. Watch what will happen.

Day 4

You Are . . .

Encounter the Word

Read Exodus 34:1-28

Explore the Word

Scripture is the story of God pursuing a people to be in covenant with Him. It's a story of God revealing His nature and heart to His chosen people. Today's passage is a great example of just that. Reread verses 5-7. What do they tell you about the character of God? What words are used to communicate His character?

_____

_____

_____

Notice Moses' response in verse 8. Worship! When you and I start understanding who He is and start gaining a clearer picture of Him, it can lead to only one thing—worship. In fact, one great way to worship God is to speak to Him about His character, to acknowledge and proclaim His name.

Live the Word

Read through Psalm 103. List all the attributes of God's character. After you've completed your list, pray, worshiping God for who He is. Use the words you've written down as launching points for praise and worship in prayer.

Day 5
The Residue of God

Encounter the Word
Read Exodus 34:29-35

Explore the Word
In today's reading we find Moses coming down from Mount Sinai with a new set of tablets and something more remarkable—a face that shone like the sun. Being with God changes you. It makes you different.

Our relationship with God should change us. It should impact every part of our lives and make us different. 2 Corinthians 2:15-16 says that we are "the aroma of Christ among those who are being saved and those who are perishing. To one we are the smell of death; to the other, the fragrance of life."

Our lives are to be lived as an aroma. Our lives are to be marked by a different set of values and pursuits—values and pursuits that will set us apart. The heart of evangelism is not about selling Jesus. It's about living a life that's consecrated so that those around us look at our lives and say, "There's something different about you. I want what you have."

Moses' face shone, and the people were amazed and in awe. They listened to what he had to say. He was different, unique. He had the residue of God all over him. He had been with God.

Live the Word
Who in your life do you know needs God? Pray that God would make you the fragrance of God in his or her life. One way to do that is to serve them unconditionally. Find three ways in which you can serve that person

this week, opening the door to share the life-altering message of God with them.

Entering In #10

"Show Me Your Kavod!"

Contemplation

In Exodus 33 we find Moses speaking face to face with God, "as a man speaks with his friend." Moses is enjoying intimate communion with God, like no other person before him. He is begging God to have His presence go with them, and God responds like a lover, saying, "Yes, I will send My presence with you." It's in this intimate moment that Moses cries out from his very soul, "Now show me your glory" (v. 18). Now in the English we miss the passion and power of what Moses is saying. What he's asking for is not to see God's "glory" but to see and sense something far more amazing. "Show me Your *kavod* [presence]!" he cries.

Moses is in the midst of this amazing moment, and he cries out, "Show me your ever-present presence all around me. Let me see and sense all that You are and all that You're doing in the here and now!" Moses is crying out to see and sense the living God, living and active in his world. In essence, he's crying out, *I want to see You—living and active. Show me yourself, O God!*

God is living and active, but the question is *Have you sensed His movement in your life? Have you seen Him moving in the lives of those around you? Have you seen and felt*

Red Sea moments? If you have, you've tasted the *kavod* of God, His ever-present and active presence in the world.

We've unfortunately forgotten many times that God is living. We express our journey with God as if salvation and a true relationship with Him is something we'll experience in the future: "Someday I'll get out of here and leave this old earth—and then I'll be in the presence of God with Jesus too." If our salvation is only for the future, we're missing the point. We're saved not *from* something as much as we're saved *to* something. God wants us to experience a taste of heaven and the kingdom of God now. We're experiencing healing and redemption from sin now. Jesus said, "Repent, for the kingdom of heaven is at hand." (Matthew 4:17). Jesus' listeners would have completely understood this.

Followers of Judaism acknowledge God with a special blessing, called a *berachah. "Baruch atah Adonai, Elohenu melech ha'olam."* In other words, "Holy One of blessing, Your presence fills creation." They would then add any specific blessing they wanted, for a person, an occasion, and so on. It was their way of reminding themselves that there was a God who was living and active in their world, a God whose *kavod* filled all of creation.

I don't know about you, but I need that! I need to see God more and more in my life and in the world around me. God wants to invade our lives and bring about real life change, not just for someday but for now. We need to cry out with Moses, *God, I need You here in this area of my life. I need You to act. Let me see Your* kavod *in this area of my life.*

Communication

Read and reflect on Psalm 27:4. Take a piece of paper and rewrite that verse in your own words, expressing the cry of your heart to see and sense the *kavod* of God. Then below those words begin to list areas in which you want to see God move in your life. Where do you need God to invade your life with His *kavod?* Once you're finished, take a few moments to pray through those areas you've listed.

Community

When you gather together as a group, share your rewrites of Psalm 27:4 with each other, along with your list. Spend time praying for each person in your group and a few of the areas in which he or she is seeking for God to make His *kavod* seen.

Compassion

As a group you may want to do a prayer walk through a neighborhood, at your school, or somewhere in your community. Pray for the people there, that they would see and sense the *kavod* of the living and active God in their lives, that they might come to know Him.

Day 1

Sabbath: Remembering Holiness

Encounter the Word

Exodus 35:1-3

Explore the Word

Most of us have grown up understanding that Sunday is
our day to go to church, but few really understand what
significance it has for us. We know by looking at the
New Testament that the Church gathered throughout
the week, but there was one day that they would all observe, the Sabbath. In today's passage God commands
the Israelites to observe the Sabbath or die. If you look
back to Exodus 20:8 you read the fourth commandment,
dealing with the Sabbath. Note that it's the only time
God says to "remember." That's because God wants the
Israelites to have one day when they're not defined by
what they do. A day not of working but of remembering
when they were in slavery.

Live the Word

Today the day of Sabbath is not as important to God as
is the spiritual truth that we're not defined by what we
do or don't do. God desires for us to remember Him and
what He has created for us. The Jews in Jesus' time took
this to new levels that distorted its ultimate purpose.
Take a day and observe the Sabbath. Do nothing that
day but pray, read scripture, and be with family and
friends. No movies or busy activity, but be with what
God has created.

Day 2

Is Your Gift of Your Own Free Will?

Encounter the Word

Exodus 35:4-29

Explore the Word

Before the Tabernacle building begins, there is a lot of preparation beforehand. God is asking that the Israelites give an offering that's of their own free will in order to build the Tabernacle. God displays His unconditional love for us by never forcing us to choose Him or worship Him. Throughout the Scriptures His theme of love is evident by not forcing His creation to do something apart from its own freewill. Despite the significance of the Tabernacle, He'll not force the Israelites to any choice. Today the offering God loves most and allows us to make as a freewill offering to Him is our own lives.

Live the Word

Read John 3:16. What are the gifts you give to God of your own free will? Are they gifts that are from a heart of love for Him and for what He has given you? This brings us back to our perspective on our spiritual life: Is it an obligation or an opportunity? List the gifts that you give to God in this way. Pray and search your heart for what else you might give to Him of your own free will.

Day 3

Will God Be Here?

Encounter the Word
Exodus 35:30-36:7

Explore the Word
This passage is one you need to read a few times to picture the amazing detail with which God instructs the builders. His Tabernacle where His presence will dwell needs specifics. We may never fully understand why He prescribes this blueprint, but we know it has some meaning. One thing is clear: God is building a beautiful Tabernacle to have His presence visit. It must have been an honored task to build the very place that He would be.

In the New Testament God did away with priests interceding for us and made us our own priesthood. He also did away with the physical Temple and created the plans for a new one. He called it the Church.

Live the Word
Have you ever thought of your church body as a beautiful tabernacle that's built with one prestigious material—people?

Read Ephesians 2:19-22. How do you treat the church you attend? Do you see your church as people who make up a holy tabernacle where God's presence is, or a lifeless building made up of brick and mortar? Take some time to reflect on all the people who make up your church body, and thank God for them.

Day 4

God Loves Our Best

Encounter the Word
Exodus 36:8-39

Explore the Word
This passage continues our look into the building of the Tabernacle. We can see the detail that God calls for in every part of its construction. Did God care about how good a job the craftsmen did? I believe He cares about what the heart of our effort is. He cared about the love and energy put into the building, and He'll take care of the results. Too many times we can get caught up in the results and think that they're a reflection of our effort—when really God is in charge of the results. We're asked only to give our best.

Live the Word
Read 2 Timothy 2:14-16; Matthew 6:20-22; and Matthew 22:36-38. What does God ask of us? If you were to put a gauge of excellent effort on your life for God, what would it read? Take this week to give your best for God in all you do.

Day 5

What Image Does God Choose for Himself?

Encounter the Word

Exodus 37:1-29

Explore the Word

Perhaps the focal point of the entire Tabernacle was the ark. It was a 4' x 2' x 2' box made of acacia wood and overlaid with gold. The lid was made of solid gold. The ark in the Tabernacle was different than any other. God desired that no image be created to attempt to describe His image but to place in the ark a copy of the Ten Words to let all people know that the cornerstone of the relationship between the Israelites and her God was the written covenant.

Live the Word

God asks that we have no graven images or idol worship but that He is known for His covenant or promises. His promise to us is His Son, Jesus Christ. How do you see God? Is He some image, or do you recognize Him for what He has promised to us?

Entering In #11

Are You Willing?

Contemplation

As we reflect on the week's readings, we can see that
God is busy building a place for His presence to be for
the Hebrews. But as noted earlier, He had some preparation to accomplish before the work would start. You see,
God caused the Egyptians to give away to the Hebrews
all the necessary materials to build the Tabernacle (Exodus 25:1-7) but would not demand them back. Even
though the Hebrews did not earn or deserve the gifts of
precious gold, silver, jewels, linens, and woods, God still
wants hearts. He cared more for the willing hearts of
the Israelites than the earthly materials they possessed.

Communication

God today still does not care about what we bring—He
wants our hearts. This picture of the Tabernacle supplies
being collected come to a beautiful climax in 36:6-7.
Moses is asked to tell the people to stop giving! There's
plenty to build the Tabernacle with. It's is an amazing
picture of those who had hearts that were willing,
which caused them to give. This is a great preparation
for what the Church is to be like today. It's intended to
be a place where Christ followers are giving their hearts
to God and are willing to give back whatever He has
given them.

Compassion

God wants your heart—nothing more. Read John 3:16; Romans 10:9-10; Ephesians 6:5-7; and 1 Thessalonians 2:3-5. Are you willing to give your heart fully to God? Now read Acts 2:42-47. What are these New Testament church founders giving? How much of your heart are you giving to the Church? This week meet with one of the pastors of your church, and ask him or her for areas toward which you can begin to give your heart.

Day 1

Reflecting on the Journey

Encounter the Word
Read Exodus 38:1-31

Explore the Journey
From here on out to the end of the Book of Exodus, the people of Israel are completing the building of the Tabernacle. With the gifts from the people, carried all the way from Egypt, they begin the process of building and erecting the Tabernacle of God in their midst, solidifying their identity as the people of God.

For the next few days we'll be reflecting on the sacred journey that the Israelites went through, from a people held in slavery to a nation, set apart and consecrated—a people in covenant with God, changed forever. We'll also be reflecting on our own sacred journey, discovering more deeply who we are and who God is.

What impacted you the most about the sacred journey of the nation of Israel?

Live the Journey
How will this change the way you live?

Day 2

Reflecting on the Journey of the Israelites

Encounter the Word
Read Exodus 39:1-21

Explore the Journey

1. How would you describe the changes that took place in the life of the Israelites during their journey?

2. What were some of the lessons the nation of Israel learned about God?

3. How did those lessons change them?

Live the Journey
How do the lessons learned by the Israelites apply to your life?

Day 3

Reflecting on the Journey of Moses

Encounter the Word
Read Exodus 39:22-43

Explore the Journey

1. Think about Moses' life in the Book of Exodus. What lessons did he learn?

2. How would you describe his relationship with God?

3. What did you learn about yourself through the life of Moses?

Live the Journey
How will you apply what you've learned?

Day 4

Reflecting on God in the Journey

Encounter the Word
Read Exodus 40:1-34

Explore the Journey

1. What important insights did you gain about who God is through this journey through the Book of Exodus?

2. What surprised you about God?

3. How did your view of Him change over the course of the journey?

4. How did this journey awaken you to the story of Jesus?

Live the Journey
How will your discoveries about God impact your life?

Day 5

Reflecting on Your Own Journey

Encounter the Word
Read Exodus 40:34-38

Explore the Journey

1. How would you have described your relationship with God before this journey through Exodus?

2. What are the main three things you learned about yourself through this journey?

3. What did you learn about being a part of community?

4. How would you describe your relationship with God now?

Live the Journey
What do you need to do to continue this sacred journey with God?

Entering In #12

The Vow

Contemplation

The close of the Book of Exodus is marked by a phrase. Eight times in the last chapter of Exodus it's mentioned of Moses that he did "as the LORD commanded" (40:16, 19, 21, 23, 25, 27, 29, 32.) Nothing pleases the heart of God more than a person who openly says, *Speak, God, and I'll do whatever You ask.* People with that kind of reckless obedience are dangerous.

The Nazirite Vow

Num. 6:1-21 captures the heart of a recklessly obedient follower. It speaks of a man or woman who wants to make a voluntary, "special" vow—one that will set him or her apart. The vow has three distinctive elements to it. First he or she must not drink wine nor eat grapes, raisins, or anything else from the vine. Second, he or she must not touch or be near a dead body. Third, the person must not cut his or her hair. Sounds crazy? Maybe. Maybe not!

The vow of the Nazirite was a voluntary one that changed the way a person looked at life and how he or she lived his or her life. You have to understand that wine was everywhere in Middle East cultures—weddings, funerals, social events, even religious events. Dead bodies? No problems for us today, but back then people were surrounded by death. People were born and died in their homes. And since generations of families lived with each other, death was more common than we experience today. All this meant that to take on a Nazirite vow, one would have to rethink his or her entire system of life. Every day, every situation had to be thought through. *Will this make me unclean?*

If a person were able to finish his or her vow, he or she would have to bring an enormous amount of offerings to the priest, more than any other offering outlined in the Old Testament, more than the ordinary person could ever afford. In fact, often the community needed to jump in and help the person finish his or her vow.

Sound odd? Maybe. Maybe not!

The Jesus Vow

What's amazing is the similarity between the vow of the Nazirite and the "Jesus vow"—the one taken to be a follower of Him. Both force us to radically alter how we live our lives. Both are costly. Both are very, very public, as long hair was not the norm back then. Both vows made the person stand out, marked as different. Both are a sign of desperation, crying out to God, *I need You so bad that I'll do anything and go without anything—because I must have more of You in my life.*

Doesn't sound so crazy, does it?

Communication

Kind of makes you wonder if Jesus and His followers ever together watched someone fulfill a Nazirite vow. It might bring just a little more power to the words of Jesus in Mark 8:34: "If anyone would come after me, he must deny himself and take up his cross and follow me." Take a few moments to read and reflect on Mark 8:34-

38. How does it make you feel? How does the passage move you? Push you? Challenge you? Make a vow, a voluntary and "special" vow, to follow God—through the good and the bad.

Community

Once you're with your group this week, share a few insights from the week's reflections on the sacred journey of the Israelites, as well as your own. Reflect on the Nazirite vow. Just as it sometimes required the community to help fulfill the vow, how can the community help you in meeting the "Jesus vow"?

The End? Or Just the Beginning?

Are we at the end? Or just the beginning? We may be at the end of this chapter in the journey, but we are far away from our true destination. Our true destination lies a little further along the road.

For the Israelites, God could have transported them directly to the Promised Land, their destination, but He chose not to. The journey is as important as the destination. Without the journey, the destination becomes just another legalistic trophy. The journey is not a means to a destination, but a means to a true end—to be more like God. To not learn from the experience of the journey is to arrive at the destination incomplete.

We can look at it one of two ways. We can focus on the destination, the end, and miss everything along the way. Or we can find joy and freshness in the midst of the journey. We can live our lives blind to the journey, focusing solely on the prize ahead, or we can find beauty in the sometimes harsh sand of the desert.

Welcome to the journey...

To your journey.